Key Facts™ on

Vietnam

~*Essential Information on Vietnam*~

By Patrick W. Nee

The Internationalist®

www.internationalist.com

The Internationalist®

International Business, Investment, and Travel

Published by:

The Internationalist Publishing Company

96 Walter Street/ Suite 200

Boston, MA 02131, USA

Tel: 617-354-7722

www.internationalist.com

PN@internationalist.com

Copyright © 2013 by PWN

Table Of Contents

Chapter 1: Background

The conquest of Vietnam by France began in 1858 and was completed by 1884. It became part of French Indochina in 1887. Vietnam declared independence after World War II, but France continued to rule until its 1954 defeat by communist forces under Ho Chi MINH. Under the Geneva Accords of 1954, Vietnam was divided into the communist North and anti-communist South. US economic and military aid to South Vietnam grew through the 1960s in an attempt to bolster the government, but US armed forces were withdrawn following a cease-fire agreement in 1973. Two years later, North Vietnamese forces overran the South reuniting the country under communist rule. Despite the return of peace, for over a decade the country experienced little economic growth because of conservative leadership policies, the persecution and mass exodus of individuals - many of them successful South Vietnamese merchants - and growing international isolation. However, since the enactment of Vietnam's "doi moi" (renovation) policy in 1986, Vietnamese authorities have committed to increased economic liberalization and enacted structural reforms needed to modernize the economy and to produce more competitive, export-driven industries. The communist leaders, however, maintain control on political expression and have resisted outside calls to improve human rights. The country continues to experience small-scale protests from various groups - the vast majority connected to land-use issues, calls for increased political space, and the lack of equitable mechanisms for resolving disputes. Various ethnic minorities, such as the Montagnards of the Central Highlands and the Khmer Krom in the southern delta region, have also held protests.

Chapter 2: People and Society

Nationality:

noun: Vietnamese (singular and plural)

adjective: Vietnamese

Ethnic groups:

Kinh (Viet) 85.7%, Tay 1.9%, Thai 1.8%, Muong 1.5%, Khmer 1.5%, Mong 1.2%, Nung 1.1%, others 5.3% (1999 census)

Languages:

Vietnamese (official), English (increasingly favored as a second language), some French, Chinese, and Khmer, mountain area languages (Mon-Khmer and Malayo-Polynesian)

Religions:

Buddhist 9.3%, Catholic 6.7%, Hoa Hao 1.5%, Cao Dai 1.1%, Protestant 0.5%, Muslim 0.1%, none 80.8% (1999 census)

Population:

92,477,857 (July 2013 est.)

country comparison to the world: 14

Age structure:

0-14 years: 24.6% (male 11,931,623/female 10,807,661)

<u>15-24 years</u>: 18.4% (male 8,796,395/female 8,215,536)

<u>25-54 years</u>: 44.4% (male 20,554,252/female 20,551,460)

<u>55-64 years</u>: 7% (male 2,936,340/female 3,517,538)

<u>65 years and over</u>: 5.6% (male 1,986,839/female 3,280,213) (2013 est.)

Median age:

<u>total</u>: 28.7 years

<u>male</u>: 27.6 years

<u>female</u>: 29.7 years (2013 est.)

Population growth rate:

1.03% (2013 est.)

<u>country comparison to the world</u>: 112

Birth rate:

16.56 births/1,000 population (2013 est.)

<u>country comparison to the world</u>: 121

Death rate:

5.94 deaths/1,000 population (2013 est.)

<u>country comparison to the world</u>: 166

Net migration rate:

-0.33 migrant(s)/1,000 population (2013 est.)

<u>country comparison to the world</u>: 127

Urbanization:

urban population: 30% of total population (2010)

rate of urbanization: 3% annual rate of change (2010-15 est.)

Major cities - population:

Ho Chi Minh City 5.976 million; HANOI (capital) 2.668 million; Haiphong 1.941 million; Da Nang 807,000 (2009)

Sex ratio:

at birth: 1.12 male(s)/female

0-14 years: 1.1 male(s)/female

15-24 years: 1.07 male(s)/female

25-54 years: 1 male(s)/female

55-64 years: 0.83 male(s)/female

65 years and over: 0.62 male(s)/female

total population: 1 male(s)/female (2013 est.)

Maternal mortality rate:

59 deaths/100,000 live births (2010)

country comparison to the world: 101

Infant mortality rate:

total: 19.61 deaths/1,000 live births

country comparison to the world: 95

male: 19.97 deaths/1,000 live births

female: 19.19 deaths/1,000 live births (2013 est.)

Life expectancy at birth:

total population: 72.65 years

country comparison to the world: 130

male: 70.2 years

female: 75.4 years (2013 est.)

Total fertility rate:

1.87 children born/woman (2013 est.)

country comparison to the world: 143

Health expenditures:

6.8% of GDP (2010)

country comparison to the world: 89

Physicians density:

1.22 physicians/1,000 population (2008)

Hospital bed density:

3.1 beds/1,000 population (2009)

Drinking water source:

improved:

urban: 99% of population

rural: 93% of population

total: 95% of population

unimproved:

urban: 1% of population

rural: 7% of population

total: 5% of population (2010 est.)

Sanitation facility access:

improved:

   urban: 94% of population

   rural: 68% of population

   total: 76% of population

unimproved:

   urban: 6% of population

   rural: 32% of population

   total: 24% of population (2010 est.)

HIV/AIDS - adult prevalence rate:

   0.4% (2009 est.)

   country comparison to the world: 73

HIV/AIDS - people living with HIV/AIDS:

   280,000 (2009 est.)

   country comparison to the world: 21

HIV/AIDS - deaths:

   14,000 (2009 est.)

   country comparison to the world: 21

Major infectious diseases:

   degree of risk: high

   food or waterborne diseases: bacterial diarrhea,

   hepatitis A, and typhoid fever

   vectorborne diseases: dengue fever, malaria, Japanese

   encephalitis, and plague

   water contact disease: leptospirosis

<u>note</u>: highly pathogenic H5N1 avian influenza has been identified in this country; it poses a negligible risk with extremely rare cases possible among US citizens who have close contact with birds (2009)

Obesity - adult prevalence rate:

1.7% (2008)

<u>country comparison to the world</u>: 186

Children under the age of 5 years underweight:

20.2% (2008)

<u>country comparison to the world</u>: 35

Education expenditures:

6.6% of GDP (2010)

<u>country comparison to the world</u>: 29

Literacy:

<u>definition</u>: age 15 and over can read and write

<u>total population</u>: 94%

<u>male</u>: 96.1%

<u>female</u>: 92% (2002 est.)

School life expectancy (primary to tertiary education):

<u>total</u>: 10 years

<u>male</u>: 11 years

<u>female</u>: 10 years (2001)

Unemployment, youth ages 15-24:

<u>total</u>: 4.6%

<u>country comparison to the world</u>: 135

<u>male</u>: 4.4%

<u>female</u>: 4.9% (2004)

Chapter 3: Government and Key Leaders

Country name:

conventional long form: Socialist Republic of Vietnam

conventional short form: Vietnam

local long form: Cong Hoa Xa Hoi Chu Nghia Viet Nam

local short form: Viet Nam

abbreviation: SRV

Government type:

Communist state

Capital:

name: Hanoi (Ha Noi)

geographic coordinates: 21 02 N, 105 51 E

time difference: UTC+7 (12 hours ahead of Washington, DC during Standard Time)

Administrative divisions:

58 provinces (tinh, singular and plural) and 5 municipalities (thanh pho, singular and plural)

provinces: An Giang, Bac Giang, Bac Kan, Bac Lieu, Bac Ninh, Ba Ria-Vung Tau, Ben Tre, Binh Dinh, Binh Duong, Binh Phuoc, Binh Thuan, Ca Mau, Cao Bang, Dak Lak, Dak Nong, Dien Bien, Dong Nai,

Dong Thap, Gia Lai, Ha Giang, Ha Nam, Ha Tinh, Hai Duong, Hau Giang, Hoa Binh, Hung Yen, Khanh Hoa, Kien Giang, Kon Tum, Lai Chau, Lam Dong, Lang Son, Lao Cai, Long An, Nam Dinh, Nghe An, Ninh Binh, Ninh Thuan, Phu Tho, Phu Yen, Quang Binh, Quang Nam, Quang Ngai, Quang Ninh, Quang Tri, Soc Trang, Son La, Tay Ninh, Thai Binh, Thai Nguyen, Thanh Hoa, Thua Thien-Hue, Tien Giang, Tra Vinh, Tuyen Quang, Vinh Long, Vinh Phuc, Yen Bai

municipalities: Can Tho, Da Nang, Ha Noi, Hai Phong, Ho Chi Minh City

Independence:

2 September 1945 (from France)

National holiday:

Independence Day, 2 September (1945)

Constitution:

15 April 1992

Legal system:

civil law system; note - the civil code of 2005 reflects a European-style civil law

International law organization participation:

has not submitted an ICJ jurisdiction declaration; non-party state to the ICCt

Suffrage:

18 years of age; universal

Executive branch:

chief of state: President Truong Tan SANG (since 25 July 2011); Vice President Nguyen Thi DOAN (25 July 2007)

head of government: Prime Minister Nguyen Tan DUNG (since 27 June 2006); Deputy Prime Minister Hoang Trung HAI (since 2 August 2007), Deputy Prime Minister Nguyen Thien NHAN (since 2 August 2007), Deputy Prime Minister Vu Van NINH (since 3 August 2011), and Deputy Prime Minister Nguyen Xuan PHUC (since 3 August 2011)

cabinet: Cabinet appointed by president based on proposal of prime minister and confirmed by National Assembly

elections: president elected by the National Assembly from among its members for five-year term; last election held 25 July 2011 (next to be held in July 2016); prime minister appointed by the president from among the members of the National Assembly; deputy prime ministers appointed by the prime minister; appointment of prime minister and deputy prime ministers confirmed by National Assembly

<u>election results</u>: Truong Tan SANG elected president, percent of National Assembly vote - 97%; Nguyen Tan DUNG elected prime minister, percent of National Assembly vote - 94%

Legislative branch:

unicameral National Assembly or Quoc Hoi (500 seats; members elected by popular vote to serve five-year terms)

<u>elections</u>: last held on 22 May 2011 (next to be held in May 2016)

<u>election results</u>: percent of vote by party - NA; seats by party - CPV 458, non-party CPV-approved 38, self-nominated 4; note - 500 candidates were elected; the 496 CPV and non-party CPV-approved delegates were members of the Vietnamese Fatherland Front and were vetted prior to the election

Judicial branch:

Supreme People's Court (chief justice is elected by the National Assembly on the recommendation of the president for a five-year term)

Political parties and leaders:

Communist Party of Vietnam or CPV [Nguyen Phu TRONG]; other parties proscribed

Political pressure groups and leaders:

8406 Bloc; Democratic Party of Vietnam or DPV;
People's Democratic Party Vietnam or PDP-VN;
Alliance for Democracy
note: these groups advocate democracy but are not
recognized by the government

International organization participation:
ADB, APEC, ARF, ASEAN, CICA, CP, EAS, FAO,
G-77, IAEA, IBRD, ICAO, ICC (NGOs), ICRM,
IDA, IFAD, IFC, IFRCS, ILO, IMF, IMO, IMSO,
Interpol, IOC, IOM, IPU, ISO, ITSO, ITU, MIGA,
NAM, OIF, OPCW, PCA, UN, UNCTAD, UNESCO,
UNIDO, UNWTO, UPU, WCO, WFTU (NGOs),
WHO, WIPO, WMO, WTO

Diplomatic representation in the US:
chief of mission: Ambassador Nguyen Quoc CUONG
chancery: 1233 20th Street NW, Suite 400,
Washington, DC 20036
telephone: [1] (202) 861-0737
FAX: [1] (202) 861-0917
consulate(s) general: Houston, New York, San
Francisco
consulate: New York

Diplomatic representation from the US:
chief of mission: Ambassador David B. SHEAR

embassy: Rose Garden Building, 170 Ngoc Khanh
St., Hanoi
mailing address: 7 Lang Ha Street, Ba Dinh District,
Hanoi; 4550 Hanoi Place, Washington, DC 20521-
4550
telephone: [84] (4) 3850-5000
FAX: [84] (4) 3850-5010
consulate(s) general: Ho Chi Minh City

Key Leaders:

Pres.	Truong Tan SANG
Vice Pres.	Nguyen Thi DOAN
Prime Min.	Nguyen Tan DUNG
Dep. Prime Min.	Hoang Trung HAI
Dep. Prime Min.	Nguyen Thien NHAN
Dep. Prime Min.	Vu Van NINH
Dep. Prime Min.	Nguyen Xuan PHUC
Min. of Agriculture & Rural Development	Cao Duc PHAT
Min. of Construction	Trinh Dinh DUNG
Min. of Culture, Sports, & Tourism	Hoang Tuan ANH
Min. of Education & Training	Pham Vu LUAN

Min. of Finance	Vuong Dinh HUE
Min. of Foreign Affairs	Pham Binh MINH
Min. of Home Affairs	Nguyen Thai BINH
Min. of Industry & Trade	Vu Huy HOANG
Min. of Information & Communications	Nguyen Bac SON
Min. of Justice	Ha Hung CUONG
Min. of Labor, War Invalids, & Social Welfare	Pham Thi Hai CHUYEN
Min. of National Defense	Phung Quang THANH, *Sr. Lt. Gen.*
Min. of Natural Resources & Environment	Nguyen Minh QUANG
Min. of Planning & Investment	Bui Quang VINH
Min. of Public Health	Nguyen Thi Kim TIEN
Min. of Public Security	Tran Dai QUANG, *Lt. Gen.*
Min. of Science &	Nguyen QUAN

Technology	
Min. of Transport	Dinh La THANG
Chmn., Govt. Inspectorate	Huynh Phong TRANH
Chmn., Office of the Govt.	Vu Duc DAM
Chmn., State Ethnic Minorities Ctte.	Giang Seo PHU
Governor, State Bank of Vietnam	Nguyen Van BINH
Ambassador to the US	Nguyen Quoc CUONG
Permanent Representative to the UN, New York	Le Hoai TRUNG

Flag description:

red field with a large yellow five-pointed star in the center; red symbolizes revolution and blood, the five-pointed star represents the five elements of the populace - peasants, workers, intellectuals, traders, and soldiers - that unite to build socialism

National symbol(s):

yellow, five-pointed star on red field

National anthem:

name: "Tien quan ca" (The Song of the Marching
Troops)

lyrics/music: Nguyen Van CAO

note: adopted as the national anthem of the
Democratic Republic of Vietnam in 1945; it became
the national anthem of the unified Socialist Republic
of Vietnam in 1976; although it consists of two
verses, only the first is used as the official anthem

Chapter 4: Military

Military branches:

People's Armed Forces: People's Army of Vietnam
(PAVN; includes Vietnam People's Navy (with Naval
Infantry), Vietnam People's Air and Air Defense
Force, Border Defense Command) (2013)

Military service age and obligation:

18 years of age for male compulsory military service;
females may volunteer for active duty military
service; conscript service obligation - 2 years (3 to 4
years in the navy); 18-45 years of age (male) or 18-40
years of age (female) for Militia Force or Self
Defense Forces (2006)

Manpower available for military service:

males age 16-49: 25,649,738
females age 16-49: 24,995,692 (2010 est.)

Manpower fit for military service:

males age 16-49: 20,405,847
females age 16-49: 21,098,102 (2010 est.)

Manpower reaching militarily significant age annually:

male: 847,743
female: 787,341 (2010 est.)

Military expenditures:

2.5% of GDP (2005 est.)

<u>country comparison to the world</u>: 56

Chapter 5: Geography

Location:

Southeastern Asia, bordering the Gulf of Thailand,
Gulf of Tonkin, and South China Sea, as well as
China, Laos, and Cambodia

Geographic coordinates:

16 10 N, 107 50 E

Map references:

Southeast Asia

Area:

total: 331,210 sq km

country comparison to the world: 66

land: 310,070 sq km

water: 21,140 sq km

Area - comparative:

slightly larger than New Mexico

Land boundaries:

total: 4,639 km

border countries: Cambodia 1,228 km, China 1,281
km, Laos 2,130 km

Coastline:

3,444 km (excludes islands)

Maritime claims:

territorial sea: 12 nm

contiguous zone: 24 nm

exclusive economic zone: 200 nm

continental shelf: 200 nm or to the edge of the
continental margin

Climate:

tropical in south; monsoonal in north with hot, rainy
season (May to September) and warm, dry season
(October to March)

Terrain:

low, flat delta in south and north; central highlands;
hilly, mountainous in far north and northwest

Elevation extremes:

lowest point: South China Sea 0 m

highest point: Fan Si Pan 3,144 m

Natural resources:

phosphates, coal, manganese, rare earth elements,
bauxite, chromate, offshore oil and gas deposits,
timber, hydropower

Land use:

arable land: 19.64%

permanent crops: 11.18%

other: 69.18% (2011)

Irrigated land:

45,850 sq km (2005)

Total renewable water resources:

884.1 cu km (2011)

Freshwater withdrawal (domestic/industrial/agricultural):

total: 82.03 cu km/yr (1%/4%/95%)

per capita: 965 cu m/yr (2005)

Natural hazards:

occasional typhoons (May to January) with extensive flooding, especially in the Mekong River delta

Environment - current issues:

logging and slash-and-burn agricultural practices contribute to deforestation and soil degradation; water pollution and overfishing threaten marine life populations; groundwater contamination limits potable water supply; growing urban industrialization and population migration are rapidly degrading environment in Hanoi and Ho Chi Minh City

Environment - international agreements:

party to: Biodiversity, Climate Change, Climate Change-Kyoto Protocol, Desertification, Endangered Species, Environmental Modification, Hazardous Wastes, Law of the Sea, Ozone Layer Protection, Ship Pollution, Wetlands

Geography - note:

extending 1,650 km north to south, the country is only 50 km across at its narrowest point

Chapter 6: Economy

Economy - overview:

Vietnam is a densely-populated developing country that has been transitioning from the rigidities of a centrally-planned economy since 1986. Vietnamese authorities have reaffirmed their commitment to economic modernization in recent years. Vietnam joined the World Trade Organization in January 2007, which has promoted more competitive, export-driven industries. Vietnam became an official negotiating partner in the Trans-Pacific Partnership trade agreement in 2010. Agriculture's share of economic output has continued to shrink from about 25% in 2000 to less than 22% in 2012, while industry's share increased from 36% to nearly 41% in the same period. State-owned enterprises account for roughly 40% of GDP. Poverty has declined significantly, and Vietnam is working to create jobs to meet the challenge of a labor force that is growing by more than one million people every year. The global recession hurt Vietnam's export-oriented economy, with GDP in 2012 growing at 5%, the slowest rate of growth since 1999. In 2012, however, exports increased by more than 18%, year-on-year; several administrative actions brought the trade deficit back into balance. Between 2008 and 2011, Vietnam's managed currency, the dong, was devalued in excess of 20%, but its value remained stable in 2012. Foreign direct investment inflows fell 4.5% to $10.5 billion in 2012. Foreign donors have pledged $6.5 billion in new development assistance for 2013. Hanoi has oscillated between promoting growth and emphasizing macroeconomic stability in recent years. In February 2011, the Government shifted policy away from policies aimed at achieving a high rate of economic growth, which had stoked inflation, to those aimed at stabilizing the economy, through tighter monetary and fiscal control. Although Vietnam unveiled a broad, "three pillar" economic reform program in early 2012, proposing the restructuring of public investment, state-owned enterprises, and the banking sector, little perceptible progress had been made by early 2013. Vietnam's economy continues to face challenges from an undercapitalized banking sector. Non-performing loans weigh heavily on banks and businesses. In September 2012, the official bad debt ratio climbed to

8.8%, though some independent analysts believe it could be higher than 15%.

GDP (purchasing power parity):

$320.1 billion (2012 est.)

country comparison to the world: 42

$304.9 billion (2011 est.)

$287.9 billion (2010 est.)

note: data are in 2012 US dollars

GDP (official exchange rate):

$138 billion (2012 est.)

GDP - real growth rate:

5% (2012 est.)

country comparison to the world: 62

5.9% (2011 est.)

6.8% (2010 est.)

GDP - per capita (PPP):

$3,500 (2012 est.)

country comparison to the world: 169

$3,400 (2011 est.)

$3,300 (2010 est.)

note: data are in 2012 US dollars

GDP - composition by sector:

agriculture: 21.5%

industry: 40.7%

services: 37.7% (2012 est.)

Labor force:

49.18 million (2012 est.)

country comparison to the world: 13

Labor force - by occupation:

agriculture: 48%

industry: 21%

services: 31% (2012)

Unemployment rate:

4.5% (2012 est.)

country comparison to the world: 41

4.5% (2011 est.)

Population below poverty line:

11.3% (2012 est.)

Household income or consumption by percentage share:

lowest 10%: 3.2%

highest 10%: 30.2% (2008)

Distribution of family income - Gini index:

37.6 (2008)

country comparison to the world: 75

36.1 (1998)

Investment (gross fixed):

28.2% of GDP (2012 est.)

country comparison to the world: 28

Budget:

revenues: $42.14 billion

expenditures: $47.57 billion (2012 est.)

Taxes and other revenues:

30.5% of GDP (2012 est.)

country comparison to the world: 95

Budget surplus (+) or deficit (-):

-3.9% of GDP (2012 est.)

country comparison to the world: 135

Public debt:

48.2% of GDP (2012 est.)

country comparison to the world: 67

48.3% of GDP (2011 est.)

note: official data; data cover general government debt, and includes debt instruments issued (or owned) by government entities other than the treasury; the data include treasury debt held by foreign entities; the data include debt issued by subnational entities, as well as intra-governmental debt; intra-governmental debt consists of treasury borrowings from surpluses in the social funds, such as for retirement, medical care, and unemployment; debt instruments for the social funds are not sold at public auctions

Inflation rate (consumer prices):

6.8% (2012 est.)

country comparison to the world: 176

18.1% (2011 est.)

Central bank discount rate:

9% (31 December 2012)

country comparison to the world: 11

15% (31 December 2011)

Commercial bank prime lending rate:

15% (31 December 2012 est.)

country comparison to the world: 30

16.96% (31 December 2011 est.)

Stock of narrow money:

$37.05 billion (31 December 2012 est.)

country comparison to the world: 53

$32.64 billion (31 December 2011 est.)

Stock of broad money:

$153.9 billion (30 October 2012 est.)

country comparison to the world: 45

$132 billion (31 December 2011 est.)

Stock of domestic credit:

$140 billion (30 October 2012 est.)

country comparison to the world: 47

$145.7 billion (31 December 2011 est.)

Market value of publicly traded shares:

$38.2 billion (31 December 2011 est.)

country comparison to the world: 59

$26 billion (31 December 2011)

$37 billion (31 December 2010 est.)

Agriculture - products:

paddy rice, coffee, rubber, tea, pepper, soybeans, cashews, sugar cane, peanuts, bananas; poultry; fish, seafood

Industries:

food processing, garments, shoes, machine-building; mining, coal, steel; cement, chemical fertilizer, glass, tires, oil, mobile phones

Industrial production growth rate:

4% (2012 est.)

country comparison to the world: 76

Current account balance:

$-457 million (2012 est.)

country comparison to the world: 92

$201 million (2011 est.)

Exports:

$114.6 billion (2012 est.)

country comparison to the world: 35

$96.91 billion (2011 est.)

Exports - commodities:

clothes, shoes, electronics, seafood, crude oil, rice, coffee, wooden products, machinery

Exports - partners:

US 18%, China 11%, Japan 11%, Germany 3.7% (2011 est.)

Imports:

$114.3 billion (2012 est.)

country comparison to the world: 33

$97.36 billion (2011 est.)

Imports - commodities:

machinery and equipment, petroleum products, steel products, raw materials for the clothing and shoe industries, electronics, plastics, automobiles

Imports - partners:

China 22%, South Korea 13.2%, Japan 10.4%, Taiwan 8.6%, Thailand 6.4%, Singapore 6.4% (2011 est.)

Reserves of foreign exchange and gold:

$20.9 billion (31 December 2012 est.)

country comparison to the world: 57

$14.05 billion (31 December 2011 est.)

Debt - external:

$41.85 billion (31 December 2012 est.)

country comparison to the world: 61

$39.63 billion (31 December 2011 est.)

Stock of direct foreign investment - at home:

$75.45 billion (31 December 2012 est.)

country comparison to the world: 46

$65.35 billion (31 December 2011 est.)

Stock of direct foreign investment - abroad:

$7.7 billion (31 December 2009 est.)

country comparison to the world: 57

$5.3 billion (31 December 2008)

Exchange rates:

dong (VND) per US dollar -

20,828 (2012 est.)

20,649 (2011 est.)

18,612.92 (2010 est.)

17,799.6 (2009)

16,548.3 (2008)

Fiscal year:

calendar year

Chapter 7: Energy

Electricity - production:

117 billion kWh (2012 est.)

country comparison to the world: 32

Electricity - consumption:

104 billion kWh (2012 est.)

country comparison to the world: 33

Electricity - exports:

1.555 million kWh (2012 est.)

country comparison to the world: 86

Electricity - imports:

2.7 billion kWh (2012 est.)

country comparison to the world: 46

Electricity - installed generating capacity:

26.3 million kW (2012 est.)

country comparison to the world: 30

Electricity - from fossil fuels:

55% of total installed capacity (2012 est.)

country comparison to the world: 146

Electricity - from nuclear fuels:

0% of total installed capacity (2012 est.)

country comparison to the world: 200

Electricity - from hydroelectric plants:

45% of total installed capacity (2012 est.)

country comparison to the world: 47

Electricity - from other renewable sources:

0.1% of total installed capacity (2012 est.)

country comparison to the world: 91

Crude oil - production:

336,100 bbl/day (2012 est.)

country comparison to the world: 33

Crude oil - exports:

188,000 bbl/day (2012 est.)

country comparison to the world: 32

Crude oil - imports:

0 bbl/day (2012 est.)

country comparison to the world: 139

Crude oil - proved reserves:

4.7 billion bbl (1 January 2013 es)

country comparison to the world: 27

Refined petroleum products - production:

112,000 bbl/day (2012 est.)

country comparison to the world: 71

Refined petroleum products - consumption:

259,900 bbl/day (2012 est.)

country comparison to the world: 48

Refined petroleum products - exports:

37,050 bbl/day (2012 est.)

country comparison to the world: 65

Refined petroleum products - imports:

184,900 bbl/day (2012 est.)

country comparison to the world: 28

Natural gas - production:

9.3 billion cu m (2012 est.)

country comparison to the world: 45

Natural gas - consumption:

10.2 billion cu m (2012 est.)

country comparison to the world: 46

Natural gas - exports:

0 cu m (2012 est.)

country comparison to the world: 203

Natural gas - imports:

890 million cu m (2012 est.)

country comparison to the world: 61

Natural gas - proved reserves:

699.4 billion cu m (1 January 2012 es)

country comparison to the world: 31

Carbon dioxide emissions from consumption of energy:

112.8 million Mt (2010 est.)

country comparison to the world: 38

Chapter 8: Communications

Telephones - main lines in use:

10.175 million (2011)

country comparison to the world: 21

Telephones - mobile cellular:

127.318 million (2011)

country comparison to the world: 8

Telephone system:

general assessment: Vietnam is putting considerable

effort into modernization and expansion of its

telecommunication system

domestic: all provincial exchanges are digitalized and

connected to Hanoi, Da Nang, and Ho Chi Minh City

by fiber-optic cable or microwave radio relay

networks; main lines have been increased, and the use

of mobile telephones is growing rapidly

international: country code - 84; a landing point for

the SEA-ME-WE-3, the C2C, and Thailand-Vietnam-

Hong Kong submarine cable systems; the Asia-

America Gateway submarine cable system, completed

in 2009, provided new access links to Asia and the

US; satellite earth stations - 2 Intersputnik (Indian

Ocean region) (2011)

Broadcast media:

government controls all broadcast media exercising oversight through the Ministry of Information and Communication (MIC); government-controlled national TV provider, Vietnam Television (VTV), operates a network of 9 channels with several regional broadcasting centers; programming is relayed nationwide via a network of provincial and municipal TV stations; law limits access to satellite TV but many households are able to access foreign programming via home satellite equipment; government-controlled Voice of Vietnam, the national radio broadcaster, broadcasts on 6 channels and is repeated on AM, FM, and shortwave stations throughout Vietnam (2008)

Internet country code:

.vn

Internet hosts:

189,553 (2012)

country comparison to the world: 74

Internet users:

23.382 million (2009)

country comparison to the world: 17

Chapter 9: Transportation

Airports:

44 (2012)

country comparison to the world: 97

Airports - with paved runways:

total: 37

over 3,047 m: 9

2,438 to 3,047 m: 6

1,524 to 2,437 m: 13

914 to 1,523 m: 9 (2012)

Airports - with unpaved runways:

total: 7

1,524 to 2,437 m: 1

914 to 1,523 m: 3

under 914 m: 3 (2012)

Heliports:

1 (2012)

Pipelines:

condensate 28 km; condensate/gas 10 km; gas 216 km; refined products 206 km (2010)

Railways:

total: 2,632 km

country comparison to the world: 62

standard gauge: 527 km 1.435-m gauge

narrow gauge: 2,105 km 1.000-m gauge (2008)

Roadways:

total: 180,549 km

country comparison to the world: 26

paved: 133,899 km

unpaved: 46,650 km (2008)

Waterways:

17,702 km (5,000 km are navigable by vessels up to 1.8 m draft) (2011)

country comparison to the world: 7

Merchant marine:

total: 579

country comparison to the world: 20

by type: barge carrier 1, bulk carrier 142, cargo 335, chemical tanker 23, container 19, liquefied gas 7, passenger/cargo 1, petroleum tanker 48, refrigerated cargo 1, roll on/roll off 1, specialized tanker 1

registered in other countries: 86 (Cambodia 1, Kiribati 2, Mongolia 33, Panama 43, Taiwan 1, Tuvalu 6) (2010)

Ports and terminals:

Cam Pha Port, Da Nang, Haiphong, Ho Chi Minh, Phu My, Quy Nhon

Transportation - note:

the International Maritime Bureau reports the territorial and offshore waters in the South China Sea as high risk for piracy and armed robbery against ships; numerous commercial vessels have been attacked and hijacked both at anchor and while underway; hijacked vessels are often disguised and cargo diverted to ports in East Asia; crews have been murdered or cast adrift

Chapter 10: Transnational Issues

Disputes - international:

southeast Asian states have enhanced border surveillance to check the spread of avian flu; Cambodia and Laos protest Vietnamese squatters and armed encroachments along border; Cambodia accuses Vietnam of a wide variety of illicit cross-border activities; progress on a joint development area with Cambodia is hampered by an unresolved dispute over sovereignty of offshore islands; an estimated 300,000 Vietnamese refugees reside in China; establishment of a maritime boundary with Cambodia is hampered by unresolved dispute over the sovereignty of offshore islands; the decade-long demarcation of the China-Vietnam land boundary was completed in 2009; China occupies the Paracel Islands also claimed by Vietnam and Taiwan; Brunei claims a maritime boundary extending beyond as far as a median with Vietnam, thus asserting an implicit claim to Lousia Reef; the 2002 "Declaration on the Conduct of Parties in the South China Sea" has eased tensions but falls short of a legally binding "code of conduct" desired by several of the disputants;

Vietnam continues to expand construction of facilities in the Spratly Islands; in March 2005, the national oil companies of China, the Philippines, and Vietnam signed a joint accord to conduct marine seismic activities in the Spratly Islands; Economic Exclusion Zone negotiations with Indonesia are ongoing, and the two countries in Fall 2011 agreed to work together to reduce illegal fishing along their maritime boundary

Illicit drugs:

minor producer of opium poppy; probable minor transit point for Southeast Asian heroin; government continues to face domestic opium/heroin/methamphetamine addiction problems despite longstanding crackdowns

Map of Vietnam

Other Key Facts™ Titles

Key Facts on Iran

Key Facts on Afghanistan

Key Facts on Iraq

Key Facts on Indonesia

Key Facts on South Korea

Key Facts on France

Key Facts on the United Kingdom

Key Facts on Egypt

Key Facts on Israel

Key Facts on Mexico

Key Facts on the United States of

America

Key Facts on Turkey

Key Facts on South Africa

Key Facts on Greece

Key Facts on Japan

Key Facts on Malaysia

All Key Facts™ Titles are Available at

www.Amazon.com

THE INTERNATIONALIST®

2013

WWW.INTERNATIONALIST.COM